The MINISTRY of PHILANTHROPY

General Conference Ministerial Association
and Philanthropic Service for Institutions
Silver Spring, MD 20904

Copyright 1999 by:
    General Conference Ministerial Association
    and Philanthropic Service for Institutions
    Adventist World Headquarters
    12501 Old Columbia Pike
    Silver Spring, MD 20904

Library of Congress Cataloging-in-Publication Data
    General Conference Ministerial Association
    and Philanthropic Service for Institutions
    The Ministry of Philanthropy: A Collection of Stories
    About How Giving Changes People's Lives
    Introduction by Jeff Scoggins
    Library of Congress Catalog Number: 99-74137

ISBN 0-9643585-2-2

# Dedicated to

Milton Murray, whose vision and passion for philanthropy continue to be an inspiration to so many people whose lives have been changed by his ministry in philanthropy.

# In Appreciation

Thank you to all who participated in this project, especially the authors who, in a true philanthropic spirit, wrote these stories and allowed them to be published in book form free of charge.

Thank you also to the staff of the Philanthropic Service for Institutions (PSI), Ken Turpen, Pam Sadler, Chris Bearce, Randy Fox, and Jo-Anne Vizcarra, all of whom work tirelessly for this ministry.

And thank you to PSI's board members—professionals with full-time jobs at other organizations—who volunteer significant time to PSI and its mission: Bj. Christensen, Jackie Bragaw, David Colwell, LuAnn Davis, Clarence Hodges, Karen Johnson, John Korb, Berney Neufeld, Dick Osborn, Juan Prestol, Brooke Sadler, and Wendy Will.

Thanks also to all you philanthropy professionals who work in advancement, development, and fund raising who understand the impact your ministry is having on others. People will be in heaven because of your work.

PSI is a department of the North American Division of the Seventh-day Adventist Church that works with the philanthropy programs at Adventist healthcare and educational organizations.

# Contents

# A Gift to the Future

"A handful of pine seed will cover mountains with the green majesty of forests. I too will set my face to the wind and throw my handful of seed on high."

—Fiona Macleod

When I began my work at Philanthropic Service for Institutions (PSI) at the Seventh-day Adventist Church, I thought I understood the meaning of the word philanthropy. I soon discovered, however, that the word is packed with profound philosophy and meaning that many of us never grasp.

I was green out of college when Milton Murray hired me at PSI. The essence of the job description he gave me my first day at work was, "Your job is to help the world understand philanthropy. Go do it." That meant that, to avoid being a hypocrite, I had to learn to understand philanthropy myself.

I must admit that at the time I had a few misgivings about philanthropy, which I considered little more than a nice word for fund raising—"begging" I have muttered on occasion.

Milton retired soon after bringing me to PSI. I think he simply stopped receiving a paycheck, however, because he still comes to my office as often as before. And I'm glad he hasn't faded away from this ministry he almost single-handedly built in the Adventist church. It's partly his influence that keeps me delving deeper into the philosophy of philanthropy and searching for new ways to illustrate its ministry.

From him I learned that giving someone else an opportunity to give is a ministry in itself. Philanthropy, like planting a tree, is an investment in the future.

*Jeff Scoggins*

The following stories are collected from several years of the column "Philosophy of Philanthropy" that runs in PSI's newsletter, *The Philanthropic Dollar.*

# I Lived in Iowa, and I Didn't Plant a Tree

Jeff Scoggins

Nebraska is flat, brown, and treeless. I knew because I had lived in neighboring Iowa for a couple of years and it boasted the same lack of beauty as Nebraska. For a Tennessee boy, used to the Great Smoky Mountains and millions of trees, Nebraska and Iowa were both downright depressing places to be. While in Iowa I would have planted some trees had I thought I was going to live there long enough to enjoy them. But trees take forever to grow, and I expected to leave soon. I *wanted* to leave soon—Iowa was a horribly boring place.

I did leave Iowa and went to high school somewhere else. As I finished my senior year, I began thinking of where to go to college. I chose Nebraska. My friends were going to Pacific Union College or Walla Walla College. They just couldn't understand why I wanted to go to Nebraska. Truth is, I couldn't understand why I decided to go to Nebraska. I had experienced Iowa. I knew better.

No place feels more like home to me than mountains and forests. I just couldn't see the appeal of dodging the local sow to fish bluegill in her murky water hole. And would backpacking be the same when I hung my food high in a windmill, away from vicious cows who might wander into my campsite during the night?

On the other hand, since everyone loves beautiful places I felt fairly confident of the absence of people. That did appeal to me, so, trees or not, Nebraska it was.

We crossed the Nebraska state line and I realized my mistake. Waist-high wheat, interrupted by the occasional silo, greeted me with numbing endlessness.

Four years, I thought to myself. Can I take this for four years? I closed my eyes and went to sleep to stop the brain over-load I was getting from counting telephone poles. Then I woke up in heaven. Huge leafy trees surrounded me. Squirrels chased each other over the lush green grass, and a few students lay on blankets in the sun, their books discarded nearby. I caught a glimpse of a sign among the trees just before we turned—Union College?

I thought Union College was in Nebraska. But this wasn't Nebraska—there were trees. Big, old trees. Old enough that the man who planted them knew he wouldn't live to see this beautiful arboretum. What kind of person dreamed that this small knoll on the endless prairie could have trees like this? And who would do it for me to enjoy?

Thank you everyone who plants a tree when you know you will never sit under its shade or enjoy its beauty. Yes, Iowa can be a horribly boring place. Forgive me for living there and not planting a tree.

# Bushwhacked by Generosity

Kim Peckham

I can't remember his name. I was about to tell you a story about an old friend, and every time I try to recall his name, my brain sends back the message, "File not found."

My brain is insolent that way. It refuses to remember anything except advertising jingles and the theme to "Gilligan's Island." I have come to my brain on bended knee saying, "Please, could you find somewhere in those billions of neurons to store my telephone calling card number?" It says, "Sorry, I just used the last of the space for a McDonald's jingle, 'Two all-beef patties, special sauce, lettuce, cheese, etc.'" I say, "I don't need to know. I'm a vegetarian!"

Some of us have photographic memories. Some of us wish we did. It reminds me of that bumper sticker that says, "If I could remember your name, I'd ask you where I left my keys." But that's enough about my poor memory.

I want to talk about my friend. He was about the best friend I had at the time. I had moved to Orlando for one year to finish an internship in public relations. He also came from out of town to work on his MBA. We were both single guys, so we'd get together to do single-guy stuff. We'd drive around the city trying to make the car tires squeal. Or we'd go to the airport and admire the Lufthansa stewardesses.

We also went to a jazz concert. Which brings me to my favorite memory of what's-his-name. The concert was held at a high school gymnasium. Wooden floors and folding chairs. The school jazz band did the warm-up, and then somebody good came on later. It was a benefit to raise money for new uniforms for the football team or some such thing.

The tickets were cheap. I think we paid two bucks. We were walking away from the ticket window when my friend paused. He turned back to the girl with the tickets. "Could I have gotten a discount with a student I.D.?" he asked.

"Ah, yes," she said. "But it all goes to a good cause."

"In that case," my friend replied, "have another dollar." He reached into his wallet and slipped a bill through the ticket window. His action caught me so much by surprise that I burst out laughing. The girl laughed too. We had been bushwhacked by generosity. For one second, the world where we each protect our little pile of money as if it were an only child was turned upside-down by a guy who said, "Have some more of mine."

So when I remember my friend, I remember him as generous, witty, and noble. And because I remember him at his best, perhaps he will forgive me for not remembering his name.

# Net Pay + Selfishness = Happiness?

Gary Krause

Pay slips are depressing. How many times have you studied the minute details, trying to figure how the gross payment shrinks into such a small net amount (the little bit you actually get to use)?

A crippling amount goes in taxes—for the police force, the nation's defense, education, and overseas junkets for politicians. (Of course, there's also social security—soon to be renamed social insecurity—and an endless array of other deductions.)

## Net Pay

If we believe all the ads that are thrust in our faces, our net pay is supposed to be the means to happiness. With our net pay we can buy dream vacations, luxury houses, and fancy cars. Then we get to smile a lot. Some people swallow this myth and spend their lives trying to increase their net pay. Often these myth-swallowers discover too late that they have, in fact, spent their lives. They're not smiling a lot. They then run around frantically chasing New Age gurus and therapists, trying to find where their lives have gone.

Other people don't buy the myth that net pay plus selfishness equals happiness. They realize that compassion and other spiritual values are more valuable parts of the equation. They discover a strange thing about money—it's rewarding when used to help other people.

## Net Life

Imagine if each month we received a life slip along with our pay slip. It would list our entire quota of life for a month—which just happens to be the same for everybody. Kind of nice to be even on something. Naturally, there are some universally compulsory deductions such as time for sleep, meals, and doing our annual tax returns. What's left over from the required stuff is the net amount—our net life.

Some people spend their net life as if there were no tomorrow. This has been a popular approach through the centuries— eat, drink, and be merry for tomorrow we die. It's like a piece of graffiti on a city wall: "Live. Consume. Die."

Others decide they want a better return from their lives. They even take steps to make sure they'll be around to collect their monthly life slips in the years ahead. They also discover what shouldn't really be a secret: time, like money, is most rewarding when used for helping others.

## Precious Resources

Jesus had a lot to say about our net pay and our net life—just glance through His parables. He says they're precious gifts, and it's important what we do with them. Philanthropy professionals who follow His teachings have a challenging task: to help people let Christian values and priorities shape the way they use their net pay and their net lives. Now that's an exciting task (unlike reading our pay slips).

# Could I Have Some Water?

Rick Kajiura

As the hot Indian sun beats down on us, I check the small plastic bottle of carefully boiled and filtered water hanging from my belt. When my wife Robyn and I left the Pune train station early this morning, the bottle seemed big and heavy with water.

But now, more than seven hours later, we climb among the ruins of a mountain fortress in the midday heat, and the bottle seems small, the remaining water meager. The water level has dropped below the halfway point, and I resist the urge to drink, unsure of how long we will be at the fortress. I am all too aware of the hot, dusty trek back down the mountain. To make matters worse, we haven't met the hikers from the Spicer College Bible camp as we planned, so we have to find the campsite on our own.

From our vantage point we spot a hawk

circling below us. Rhesus and langur monkeys scamper on dry cliffs as we turn and walk back toward the trail.

At first I can't understand what he is saying. We met him on the trail—a young Indian man looking as hot and tired as I feel. Dressed in a traditional dhoti, he speaks again and points, "Paanee?"

"He wants water," Robyn says. "Give him the bottle."

A million thoughts, a million objections crowd my mind: We don't have much water left. We don't know when we will find more. I've been carrying it all this time for us, why didn't he carry his own water? What if he's sick? We might catch it. What if he drinks it all?

Silently I hand Robyn the bottle and watch as she hands it to the man. He drinks as I've seen others do, pouring the water into his mouth without touching the rim, without seeming to swallow. He drinks only a little, as though recognizing the value of what we are giving him. Returning the bottle and smiling, he thanks us and continues up the path.

Over the years, I've been asked to give many gifts—of both time and money.

Sometimes I say yes, and sometimes I say no. But now and again I think about that Indian mountaintop and the values I have. Here in North America, where I get water simply by turning a tap, I can give away gallons of water. But on that scorching day in India, I was tempted to deny a man a couple of ounces of my water.

Remembering the mountaintop, I realize that it isn't what I give or how much that's important, but what the gift means and what it can do—not only for a thirsty man but also for me.

# An Opportunity for Blisters

Jeff Scoggins

I lived in Rwanda several years before
the civil war broke out there. When we first
arrived I lived with my parents, brother, and
sister up at the Seventh-day Adventist university. Mudende, as it was called, is nestled
in the green mountains about a two-hours'
drive from Kigali, the capital. We were at
the university to study the language for a
couple of months before moving down to
Kigali, where my parents were to work.

After a few grueling lessons in
Kinyarwanda (the seventh hardest language in the world) I convinced my parents that since I was heading off to boarding school in Kenya soon, I really didn't
need to learn this language. If anything, I
should learn Swahili. They finally agreed
and switched me to French. Swahili wasn't
available. That wasn't what I had in mind,
though. In fact, studying of any kind was
out of the question. So after two lessons I

somehow managed to squirm out of French classes as well to do what I really wanted to do—kick around with a dozen new friends from as many different countries doing absolutely nothing. Well, that lasted for a couple of weeks until my dad finally offered me an "opportunity."

You see, the university ran a farm large enough to keep the French Foreign Legion in potatoes for life. I wasn't sure if my dad was aware of this when he came to me, but it turns out he did.

"Jeff," he asked, "how much money do you have to take to school?" I was 14 years old with a minimal allowance, so the blank stare I returned was perfectly appropriate.

"Well, then," he continued, "how would you like to earn some money for school working on the farm?" It was phrased like a question, but it wasn't.

"How much do they pay?" I asked.

"About $1.50..." he said.

I started counting fingers. "$1.50 times eight hours...."

"...per day," my dad finished his sentence.

If it had been anyone else besides my

dad I'd have laughed at him. What an amazing opportunity! Hoe potatoes for a solid eight hours for $1.50![1]

The next morning at 7 a.m. I stood with a crowd of others to receive my work assignment, as I would do every morning for the next couple of weeks. Oh, if only I could describe what I thought of my opportunity—my opportunity for hand blisters the size of small jellyfish, my opportunity for backaches a 14-year-old had never known, and my opportunity to pocket a whole $22.50. It wasn't worth it.

However, looking back, I've changed my mind. I should be grateful they paid me at all. Really, I might just as well have paid the farm for allowing me to work. What those back breaking days in the potato fields paid me was a kind of payment I can't very well describe. Opportunity to sleep the sleep of the exhausted-but-happy. Opportunity to see blisters turn to callouses. Opportunity to see and be satisfied with what I accomplished.

Aren't those the best kinds of opportunities to receive? They're also the best kind to give. Thanks, Dad.

[1] Maybe sometime I'll tell you about my opportunity to pick rat droppings out of rice for two bags of it (rice) per month.

# Going Once, Going Twice...

Sophie Anderson

The pungent scent of apple pie lured me to the oven. Wincing, I creaked open the metal door, heat waves blasting my face, and peered inside. There it lay, its apple ooze bubbling from a blackened crust, its face hardened into brick. Once again I was defeated. So when the phone rang later, I wasn't prepared.

"Will you bake a pie for our pie auction Saturday night?" asked one of my students in the school where I taught. "We're trying to raise money for our senior trip." I paused. Such a little request. But the words "bake" and "pie" launched me into a spinning culinary orbit.

"No!" my good sense screamed. "I'd love to," I lied. I put down the receiver. What have I done? The reason I couldn't bake a normal pie was as cloudy as why I'd agreed to do it in the first place.

Try a box recipe, my logical mind suggested. No. Too tacky. Why not buy one? I tried again. But that's cheap. My students deserve more than a store-bought pie.

Friday afternoon I found my smudged recipe. A delicious recipe when others used it, at my touch the ingredients conspired against me. But today this was more than pie; it was a fire-breathing challenge. Later, however, pulling the pie out of the oven, I groaned. Maybe I'll buy one after all, I sighed, hopeless and out of time.

Saturday night came and the pie remained unmade. With no time to get to town, I found the ingredients again, resolute. With only minutes, I launched myself into a carnage-strewn battlefield of apple cores, flour, and sticky dishes. When my pie was barely in the oven, the clock shrieked time for the performance before the auction. Setting a mental timer, I left the pie to its baking fate and rushed out the door. Luckily I lived close enough to hurry back and take it out of the oven. Maybe.

I watched the performance and my watch with equal fervor, then rushed out with few minutes to spare. I eased the pie out, wanting to at least taste it, but there was no time.

In the auditorium once more, I surrendered the pie to official hands and melted back into the audience. The bidding began. $10, $15, $20. I swallowed. I didn't expect it would go this high. From a battalion of perfect pies, mostly store-bought, they described each one, praising its characteristics and details.

"Wow! Still steaming hot from the oven, folks, fresh apple pie—like grandma bakes—" The auctioneer's words jolted me from my pastry ponderings. He held an ordinary pie, laced in semiperfect crust. To me, however, it was beautiful, crowned with appled glory, a princess of piedom, mine! $30, $40, $50. Sold! It took me several minutes to recover.

The store-bought pies, I discovered, though perfect and tasty, rarely sold for a high price like the homemade ones. I learned that gifts straight from the heart, like my pie from the oven, no matter how clumsy or novice, carry the highest bid.

As I slipped out into the crisp winter air, I knew my giving had heated more than my kitchen, baked more than my students budget, and melted more than someone's ice cream. Besides giving me hope for my future grandkids, it had warmed my life. Though I never had a bite, I still savor the taste of that pie.

# Gift in a Brown Paper Bag

Jeff Scoggins

I'm recently married. A year ago actually. And I've learned about a lot of things, one of which is food. Gone are the days of categorizing meals by color. No more popping the top off a can of beans and slapping it directly on the stove. No more grabbing a handful of potato chips when I don't have time for breakfast. Now it's a refrigerator that not only has food in it, but food that will go bad in under six months.

I've discovered something else too— ingredients and Recommended Daily Allowance (RDA). Did you know that the good taste of food is directly proportional to the unpronounceability of its ingredients and the slaughter of its RDA percentages? It seems my food choices during my unenlightened bachelor years more closely resembled the periodic tables (i.e. Na, Msg, Fat) than the food pyramid.

I discovered also that color categorizing my food was a good idea—except you're supposed to have all colors, every meal, with heavy emphasis on the green ones. "Well, okay," I argued, "I'll get a seven layer burrito at Taco Bell rather than the bean and cheese. Seven layers have lettuce *and* tomatoes."

Well, long story short, I carry a brown paper bag to work now, and Taco Bell employees respond to my "The usual" with humorous confusion.

Let me say here that my wife, Becky, is the best thing that ever happened to me, and that includes her healthy food, which is scrumptious by everyone's standards.

However, the other day she forgot to send me a lunch. I considered mentioning it, but, being a liberated male, I didn't want to presume she should always cook for me. In other words: periodic tables, here I come.

When I got to work an e-mail from Becky awaited me, the essence of which was, "Oh no, I forgot to send your lunch! That means you're going to eat unhealthy food. Well, just remember, it may taste good, but it doesn't have any love in it."

The cafeteria was serving my favorite that day, an American buffet. Burgers, hot dogs, fries, etc. I even forgot salad. (I really did forget.) And, honestly, I enjoyed my food. But it took a conscious effort because my wife's words echoed in my mind, "It doesn't have any love in it."

I have a gift in a brown bag again today. I don't even know what it is yet. But I don't care if it's squash, eggplant, and stuffed green peppers, I'm going to relish it. I don't want to lose the significance of that gift by taking it for granted, by feeling it's not enough, by thinking I deserve it, or by not taking time to give back.

# The Choir Dress

John Deming

Mention the word "philanthropist" and one's mind turns to names famous and faces familiar. Large sums of money for well-known causes or institutions. Call the person who gives $10 or volunteers at a soup kitchen "philanthropist" and a look of incredulity might spread across their face.

At phonathon time we ask students to help call our alumni to see if they would be willing to give this year. For this privilege we provide supper in addition to a small monetary sum as an expression of thanks. Last year Sue (not her real name) was one of those students. She was a freshman and the oldest of five children in a single-parent home, working the summer and school year to help pay her tuition. What teenager couldn't use some extra dollars?

The calling began and soon Sue's cheerful and friendly voice encouraged alumni to give gifts large and small. A bit nervous at first, she came to see the purpose of calling and even enjoyed making contacts.

At evening's end Sue's eyes sparkled as she received her money. But then the unexpected happened. Could she make a contribution? If others had given, why shouldn't she? And with that, she returned a portion of her earnings. But the story doesn't end there.

Sue was a member of the school choir for which the young women were asked to purchase long black dresses to wear for performances. Knowing her mother didn't have the money to buy her dress, Sue began saving her extra money. She needed the dress in time for the Christmas program.

December came and Sue found out that Christmas was going to be a bit slim for her younger brothers and sisters. She finally had the money for her black choir dress, but was that the thing to do in light of upcoming Christmas?

Sue made her decision. Gifts for siblings were more important than a dress for herself.

A few days before the concert, our choir director learned of the situation and relayed the story to us in the office. "Anything we can do?"

Yes, we could do something. The school family had created a fund to assist students just when they needed a little boost of encouragement. Bible conference, varsity sports fees, maybe even a choir dress.

Are more words needed to describe the joy in the office and the look on Sue's face when she received the money for her choir dress?

All gifts aren't million-dollar donations. Some are more than gifts. They are lessons. Sue taught us that.

# The Grace of Giving

Rich Carlson

As I was reading my Bible recently, I came across a most amazing section of scripture full of astounding insight on giving. 2 Corinthians 8 and 9 contain some of Paul's counsel to the Christian believers in Corinth regarding their giving patterns: how they compared to last year, how they compare to other churches, and how they compare to God's ideal. I was intrigued by the concepts I discovered in this philosophy of giving.

Apparently the people in that very affluent city used to have a rather positive view of giving. They not only gave generously but wanted to give. Verse 11 even talks about their "eager willingness" to give. But something changed. They now were having to be talked into giving. What do you do with a change of heart in your regular givers?

Paul saw value in encouraging the people in Corinth to give by illustrating the attitude of others who were giving. He talked about those in the Macedonian church as people who, though in extreme poverty, not only gave, but urgently pleaded for the privilege to give. Now there is a concept that would thrill the heart of any fund raiser! Could you imagine expending your creative powers, not toward a new method to encourage giving, but toward controlling crowds who were knocking at your door pleading for the chance to give to your cause?

The ideal picture of giving painted by Paul seems to be done in hues of attitude more than amplitude, what is in the heart rather than what is in the checkbook. The Macedonians had accomplished their positive giving patterns because they gave themselves first to the Lord and then to others. Paul stressed the concept of equality, that when I have plenty it is my opportunity to invest in those who have less, so that if and when I have less they might provide from their plenty. He focuses on giving, not as a sacrifice at all, but as an investment in and preparation for an expected harvest. He directs us toward the idea that if we have been provided with riches, it is so we can be generous and use those riches to express our thanks to God.

Are we fund raisers or are we awareness raisers? Is our goal to raise money or to raise awareness of God's grace in giving His Son, and through Him, the plan of salvation to all people? Do we want people to give to us or to give to God? Who do we hope gets the credit (or glory) from the efforts that we put forth? Do we really believe that it all belongs to God anyway and our task is not so much opening checkbooks as opening hearts? Will checkbooks open for the right reason if we can open eyes and hearts to the opportunity to invest in God's harvest and not in our goals? I believe they will.

# Angels in Bangkok

Lynnetta Siagian Hamstra

My heart pounded, my breathing was erratic, my arms ached, and my legs were ready to buckle as I ran from one terminal to the other through the connecting walkway. With each step, my luggage got heavier. I was in beautiful Phuket, Thailand. My meetings had ended a day earlier than planned, which gave me an extra day that I could use to visit my folks in Malaysia—if I could catch a flight out.

As I boarded the plane, airport officials instructed me to go to the Malaysian Airline office on arrival in Bangkok to get a ticket for the next plane out to Kuala Lumpur, Malaysia. They assured me I had plenty of time. When we landed in Bangkok, I didn't have much time. The helpful airport personnel told me I had to go to the next terminal and I could either wait for a bus or use the walkway, which was about a quarter of a mile long. Quarter of a mile? My foot. It was nearly a mile long. I ran and walked and ran some more. Breathless, I reached the second terminal only to be told I must go to the adjacent building. I had only minutes to spare and nobody seemed to know which direction was the fastest route.

I took off running again, nearly knocking down two young ladies in my haste. Suddenly I felt compelled to stop and ask them for directions. The young ladies (who must have been in their late teens) saw the frustrated look on my face and asked where was I going. When I quickly explained, they looked at each other and said, "We will take you there." One of them grabbed a bag and the other steered me in the right direction and we were off.

At the Malaysian Airline office I thanked my guides profusely and ran in. A few minutes later, ticket in hand, I rushed out to find that the girls were waiting patiently for me. Again they steered me in the quickest direction to the check-in counters. I waited in line only to find that I didn't have enough Thai money to pay my airport tax. I needed an ATM, quickly! I got out of line and looked around frantically. The girls were at my side in moments. They were waiting to be sure I got through with no problems. They ushered me quickly to an ATM, machine then waited discreetly off to the side as I did my transaction.

Back at the check-in counter the lady informed me that I could barely make the flight. I had to hurry. I turned around to go when one of the young ladies reminded me to pick up my wallet, which was still on the counter. "Thank you," I breathed as they ushered me off to the departure gate, flashing their airport passes as we hurried past security.

I made it to the gate to find the passengers for my flight already boarding. I stopped and thanked the two young ladies from the bottom of my heart. I knew that without them I wouldn't have made the flight connection. They both smiled sweetly as we introduced ourselves to each other. One pulled out a packet of dried plums from her purse and gave it to me, saying, "Just something for you to eat on the plane."

Finally in my seat, drained from the excitement and frustration of the last few minutes, I thanked the Lord over and over again for his wonderful way of providing help when we need it. The two ladies I met were sweet, caring, honest, helpful, and giving. Asking nothing in return, they had helped a total stranger. Who were they? I like to think they were angels in Bangkok.

# A Sense of Worth

Bonnie L. Casey

The doctor called me into her office and over to a lighted panel on the wall. "Let me show you Sally's X-rays," she said soothingly, "so you'll understand the problem." Seeing my ashen countenance, she immediately added, "Don't be alarmed. She'll be alright."

The doctor pointed to an area on the X-ray. "This is Sally's heart and lungs," she explained, indicating a patch of gray with white lines radiating from it. "You can see that her blood vessels are engorged, indicating hypertension that's contributing to her respiratory difficulties."

"Yes, I see," I said, nodding sagely, not admitting that all I saw was an aerial view of a tangled freeway interchange on a particularly foggy night. "Can you help her?" I asked.

"I can give her tablets to relieve the hypertension," she answered cheerfully.

"They'll run you about a dollar a day. Sally will probably have to take them for the rest of her life."

"A dollar a day?" I cried in alarm. I looked down at the little patient on the examining table. "Sally, are you worth a dollar a day?"

Sally just said, "Woof."

I'd dreamed for years of getting a dog, spurred by memories of Rags, my child-hood pal, and by countless episodes of "Wishbone," the TV pooch. My young son and I fantasized about a sturdy little mutt who would fetch a tennis ball, catch a fris-bee, and play tug-of-war with an old slip-per.

But it was Sally who came to us through an adoption process only slightly less rigor-ous than that for adopting a child. We'd fallen in love with her at first sight, but we soon discovered she's more decorative than utilitarian. Sally is cute enough to turn heads in the park, but her vocabulary does-n't include "fetch," and she's baffled by a frisbee. She will chase an occasional cat or squirrel, but by nature and preference she's a bit of a priss.

So I spent the drive home half-seriously

counting the cost of keeping her alive. What exactly was she good for? What did she give back that was worth a dollar a day?

As Sally licked the hand nearest her nose, I realized that her only interest in life is her human family. She fusses if one of us is missing, and she runs among our feet "herding" us when we all take walks together. She greets our return at the end of the day with a squirming dance of delight and a keening little song that resembles the wail of a howler monkey more than any known canine utterance. She sleeps curled up at my feet and refuses to leave my side when I'm sick.

By the time I got home from the vet, I'd decided that devotion like that was a bargain at a dollar a day. And besides, I could hardly complain when Sally is giving so much more. She's giving all she's got.

# Wrapped in Love

Tim Lale

People have given me so many things lately.

I sat on a bench in a mall in Baltimore one day and complained to my wife about a headache. A mall employee in overalls was standing nearby emptying an ashtray stand. He must have overheard my whining, because he pulled a package out of his pocket and offered me an aspirin. He gave me the gift of relief.

Another time I walked up to the register in County Market with a 40-pound bag of dog munchies on my shoulder. The man in front of me said, "You go ahead," and stepped around me. I wanted to pay him for being so thoughtful. He gave me his spot, no questions asked.

A couple of weeks ago I bought some cereal and chocolate chips at Martin's grocery store. After adding up the prices, I thought I had enough change in my pocket to cover them. But when the cashier rang them up, I was 30 cents short. Kind of embarrassed, I said to the cashier, "I'll run across to the bank for cash."

She said, "Don't worry," and pulled out a generic $1.00-off coupon, ran it over the scanner, and gave me the change.

I shouldn't be so surprised that God still puts thoughts of generosity into the minds of many people of all ages, backgrounds, and races. He gives everyone a gift for giving in some way. When some see opportunities to give of themselves, they deliver. I want to match their gifts by passing on the blessing to others.

"So in everything, do to others as you would have them do to you, for this sums up the Law and the Prophets" (Matthew 7:12).

# The Note Posted above My Computer

Doug Nesmith

Standing in front of the surprisingly large audience, I cleared my throat and continued, "People need to hear they are appreciated. It's food for their souls!" Several people responded with a hearty "Amen."

Encouraged by this audible reply, I pressed on: "And there's more to it than just telling someone you appreciate them. Make it concrete! Why do you think teachers give gold stars when students do well? So the kids can see a result of their actions! And do you think the teachers spend a lot of money on those gold stars? Of course not!"

I could see I was really getting through to the assembly. Actually, I had thrown this talk together the night before. But for not having much of a point, my presentation was going well. "If you want to touch somebody's life, I mean really make a memory, to really create a moment they will never forget, you must give a piece of yourself. Something that matters. Something that puts you out of your way. If you want to affect someone's life, you must also affect your own life in the way you show your appreciation."

I paused for effect and was pleased to see the number of heads nodding in agreement as they pondered the depth of my thoughtful statements. Satisfied I had impressed my audience, I sat back in my seat and waited for the program to finish. Afterward, as I headed to the swimming pool, several of my classmates congratulated me on the chapel talk.

"You were good, Doug. I wish I could speak in front of groups like you!"

I blushed lightly and thanked them for their compliments, and immediately forgot everything they said, because right after you make a public speech, everyone is automatically going to compliment you, whether you really did a good job or not.

A couple of days later, I was inside an elevator with one of my professors. While we both stared at the doors (because somewhere there's a rule that you're supposed to stare at the doors when you are in an elevator), he cleared his throat and said, "That was quite a worship talk you had on Tuesday. I enjoy hearing you speak."

"Thank you, sir," I answered, and promptly forgot the compliment, because he only gave it because we were in the elevator and he probably felt that giving an unfelt, mindless compliment was better than silence.

Several weeks later a note came in the mail from the parent of an acquaintance. It read: "Thank you for your chapel talk on May 15. It had a great impact on me. God bless." Wow! He remembered what I talked about. He didn't compliment me just to start a conversation. He actually took the time to sit down, write a note, look up my address, and paste on a stamp.

As I am writing this I can remember a lot of other speeches and sermons I've given since then, and I have received compliments, gifts, and money for many of them. But only one is posted above my computer to look at every day.

You know, I have a friend who worked

for me a couple of weeks ago, just because I asked him too. I thanked him for helping me then, but right now I've got a couple of extra minutes. Maybe I'll write a thank you note of my own.

# When Mount Everest
# Goes Jogging

Byard Parks

I met a man who went to church in bor-
rowed shoes.

I was in the heart of Romania, at the
dedication of a new church. Several hundred people were milling around outside
their new white "house of prayer." The silver of the roof gleamed in the bright morning light like a mercury stream flowing from
the throne of God.

Mostly farmers and poor country folk,
the people came dressed simply, their finest
adornment being their rosy smiles, with an
occasional gleaming gold tooth. The thrill
of a new church in this so recently reli-
giously persecuted land was evident by the
pageantry that attended the ribbon cutting.
On the front steps of the church, choirs
sang, poetry was recited, speeches were
given, and tears were shed. Scarfed women

lay bouquet after bouquet of fresh-cut garden flowers on the front steps.

Amidst this colorful floral collage, my translator pointed to one quiet man standing with his worn tweed hat clasped firmly in his leathered hands.

"You see that man, Byard?" he whispered, pointing him out. "That man has dedicated the last four years of his life to building this church. He has put everything he has into making this church a reality." My friend paused and then lowered his voice even further. "He has given so much, he had to borrow shoes from a neighbor to come to church today."

Jesus says, "If you only have the faith of a mustard seed you could say to that mountain, 'Go throw yourself into the sea,' and it would be done."

How many times do we read this text and think, Wow! If only I had that kind of faith, just think what I could do! We wish for it so we could excavate a few mountains that stand in our way. We long to have that kind of faith—for our benefit. But a seed that strong is not a seed of self-willed wonders. It is strong because it is everything except self.

It is a faith that believes so strongly in the kingdom of God that it neglects itself.

It is a faith that believes so earnestly in the gospel that it lives in poverty to see the gospel advanced. It is a faith that believes so devotedly in Jesus Christ that it would go barefoot to build a house of worship.

I met a man with that kind of faith. He had a love for Jesus, a happy heart, and no shoes. What about you?

# Stuck in Paradise and Happy

Jeff Scoggins

My dad was in Cyprus on business for a few weeks, and since the island can't be more than a hundred miles from Beirut, Lebanon where we lived at the time, our whole family hopped on the plane with him. I spent my days in Cyprus making friends, building forts, getting stung by bees, and riding whoever's bicycle I could borrow.

I was too young to fully appreciate that I was in a white-sanded paradise. It was beautiful, I knew, but I assumed everyone managed to have such a lazy summer every decade or so. This was simply my first. But it has been a long time and I'm still waiting for the second.

Anyway, the day I'm thinking of was particularly gorgeous. It wasn't gorgeous because of the fighting in Beirut airport that wasn't allowing us to go home, but because school started that day and I wasn't going to be there for it. We were stuck in paradise!

Every child who hates school needs to experience the feeling of gleefully waving to friends as they plod to classes, book bags in hand. The downside that day, though, was no one wanted to lend me his bike. But finally one boy who actually liked school gave me his.

As I cruised the quiet streets of the neighborhood that morning, I was loving life. Sunshine, a bicycle, empty roads and trails, no school—what more could a boy ask for? If you'd asked, I could have told you I was happy.

As I rounded a corner that morning a grandmother and her young grandson were leaning over a tricycle on the sidewalk. They saw me and motioned me over. When I braked to a stop beside them, they showed me the back wheel of the tricycle. It was about to fall off. It only took a second to find the loose bolt, but my pickup truck full of tools wasn't due to show up for another 12 years. So I had to improvise.

I raced back to our apartment and found a stiff piece of metal, bent in just about the right shape to grip the loose bolt.

Believe it or not, it worked beautifully and I sent a grateful grandmother and grandson on their way down the sidewalk. I don't know how much reflecting I did at 10 years old, but suddenly you wouldn't have needed to ask me if I was happy. I consciously thought, "I'm happy and I like it."

As humans do when we receive a shot of happiness or quick dose of "feel-good," we go looking for more. And that's what I did that day. I went looking for someone else to help. I found her—wrinkled, bent, and dragging a gigantic load of sticks down the road. I asked if I could carry her load for her. She looked at me quizzically and said something that was Greek to me—literally. I tried again, and even attempted to take the sticks from her. But she snatched them back. I couldn't make her understand my motives weren't devious, so I finally let the poor lady go her way. At least I had tried.

I whistled as I peddled toward home. I'd be lying if I said I was pondering how helping someone else made me so happy. Neither was I philosophizing about where we usually look for happiness. Neither did I suddenly come to realize how happiness is only a gift away.

No, I was thinking nothing more than how nice it was to be stuck in Cyprus, missing school, and happy.

# It's Mine!

Kim Strobel

From an adult perspective, being a kid has great advantages. Meals bought and prepared for you. Clothes laundered. Piggy banks filled with money—sometimes earned and sometimes not. But being a kid also has its share of frustrations and challenges, and learning to share your stuff is one of them. From the time we're small we're taught to give and share with others. But, oh, it's a difficult lesson to learn.

As an adult I still lose focus and become enamored with stuff. Cars. Houses. Food. Large savings accounts. Time. It's mine—and I don't want to share my stuff.

Walla Walla College President W.G. Nelson recently shared with our office a letter he received from a Walla Walla alumnus about her five-year-old daughter. It helped me refocus on what it means to share my stuff.

Dear President Nelson,

Today we received your letter concerning fund raising for the Walla Walla College annual fund.

I asked my daughter how much money we should send. She said, "Why should we send money?" I explained that the money we send will go to help students who may not be able to pay the cost of attending Walla Walla College.

"How about $10?" she said. Then she added that she wanted to send all the money in her bank and ran to get it. She emptied the bank and quickly "counted" the money and came up with the total of $23. I counted $1.91 in pennies, nickels, dimes, and quarters.

I'm sending $23 in her name—you can be sure it comes from the heart.

Sincerely,
Julie Byard
Mother of Rebecca Byard, Class of 2014

Looking at life from Rebecca's perspective, I stopped for a moment to play "Let's Pretend." Let's pretend I had a loving parent who had always taken care of all my needs. (Hmmm, that's not a bad feeling.) Okay, given that fact, let's pretend I had something of value, like $1.91, or $1,000, or a car, or an hour I thought was worth much more (like $23), or financial security, or prestige, or a nap.

Would I be willing to share?

Looking at it from Rebecca's perspective, I think I would.

# The Lord Is So Good to Us

Don Vollmer

I was spending a few days with my mom, who lives alone in her secluded home in the mountains of western North Carolina. We were sitting at the table on her sunporch as she paid her bills and I read. I knew she was writing a check for her tithe and offerings when I heard the familiar litany, "The Lord is so good to us."

"The Lord is so good to us." How often growing up I had heard that truth from her lips as my mom returned tithe and offerings. As young adults, my brother, sister, and I had heard from my folks' admiring and wondering tax accountant, who was also a family friend, that a third of my dad's annual income went to the cause of the One who was "so good to us."

And indeed the windows of heaven were open in our home as promised. Not that we were better off financially with some material return from the Lord (my best guess is that we remained the poorer for it), but we enjoyed a domestic harmony and happiness, and a positive relationship to the church that no amount of money could ever have secured. Looking back, there did seem to be a correlation between Dad and Mom's trust and generosity and the heaven we remember in our childhood home. Our parents' gentle and good-humored nurturing over meals, around the piano, before the fire, and at play made credible Mom's repeated assertion, "The Lord is so good to us." We found security in our parents' values and learned to share in the satisfaction and delight that comes from financing mission, even if it means what some would think of as sacrifice.

Though Dad was a doctor and we could see the earning potential of his profession (I say potential because, true to his character, the time he took with each patient limited his income), when it came time for his children to choose a life's work, the question of how much money we might make at what we did, or what lifestyle we might afford for ourselves, never entered our heads. Our parents' values of mission enabled us to experience and believe for ourselves a wonderful and divine irony: sacrificial benevolence that may limit our lifestyle yields the happiest of lives, a rare contentment, and domestic tranquility. After all, the Lord is so good to us.

# Bush Benevolence 101

Jackie Ordelheide Smith

Recently, while in the Solomon Islands, I had a crash course in benevolence. My purpose in being there was to visit Global Mission Pioneers, who are establishing new congregations on the island of Malaita. My sister, Peggy, seeing an opportunity to visit the South Pacific, opted to travel with me.

Shortly after arriving at our final destination (two days later), Myna, the Malaitan nurse who worked at the clinic on the compound where we were staying, ran into our room and asked if we would like to see a baby being born. "Of course," we said as we quickly followed her out the door. "The mother is down the hill, by the field," she said in her Pidgin English. "You go ahead; I have to go by the clinic."

Peggy and I stumbled down the bumpy dirt path carved by bare feet. We crossed an open field and waited for directions. Some ladies met us and pointed us to where the mother lay. They assumed we were nurses. I was not prepared for what I saw. The mother had already given birth. She lay in a bed of weeds, just behind a bush, with the newborn on her stomach, cord still attached, and the afterbirth in a bloody pool on the ground around her. A dirty light blue cloth lay draped on the baby for warmth. The baby was wide awake and alert. Surely this isn't where she delivered!

Myna arrived seconds later and casually went to work. Fortunately she knew what to do! She unwrapped a sterilized scalpel blade, minus the handle, and cut the cord. She crimped a plastic clip on the baby's cord, wrapped the dirty blue cloth tightly around the baby, and handed her to me to hold. Caught off guard, I passed her off to my sister. Feeling too queasy, at that point, to do much more than refrain from vomiting, I stepped away to talk to the lady onlookers. The nurse, attentive only to her patient, checked to make sure all the placenta had been removed from the mother, gave the mother an injection, and matter-of-factly started digging a hole. I can't believe this! I thought. She even brought a shovel to bury the afterbirth? Who would have thought . . . ? Obviously this was not her first bush delivery.

As we walked back to the clinic to clean up the baby and weigh it, the nurse explained that many ladies choose to deliver their babies in the bush because they cannot afford the $35 fee they charge at the clinic. "When I hear about mothers who deliver this way," she said, "I go visit them anyway to make sure they are okay." Later that night, Myna went back to the mother's village to check on her.

This was no ordinary nurse. Myna and her husband, Daffie, also a nurse, have been serving in these parts for the past 30 years. They say that they are getting a little tired now and are planning to retire soon. In spite of the primitive facility in which they work, they continue to give routine and emergency care to villagers in the surrounding area who would not otherwise receive treatment. They willingly give of their time and means with little or no compensation. They offer free healthcare to those who need it, and help restore the dignity to those—like the new mother—who can't afford it. That's benevolence.

# Fun, Frustration, and Fulfillment

Kermit Netteburg

"The church wants to have Water Fun Night every Tuesday this summer. Would you be willing to bring your boat every Tuesday night from 6 to 9 p.m.?" The request was deceptively simple.

"Sure. That sounds like fun," I responded.

But every Tuesday about 5:00 p.m., when there was still just a little work I wanted to stay at the office to finish, I regretted that commitment. Some office task was just starting to come together. It was a brochure one week, a proposal another week, a review of photos for advertising yet another time. Water Fun Night was really annoying.

I began to dread Tuesday afternoons. I got tense. I got edgy. As each Tuesday afternoon wore on, so did my patience. I didn't have time to take those kids water skiing or tubing or just boat riding. By 6 p.m. when I arrived at the boat dock, my anger, my tenseness, my frustration bubbled barely below the surface.

But I kept the time commitment each week. We would load five or six teens in the boat and leave the dock. Five minutes upriver, we'd attach the tow rope, throw the tube over the side, put wetsuits and life jackets on one or two of the teens, and start the thrill rides.

Around in circles. Creating our own waves. Tossing the tube—and its occupants—into the air. Laughter filled the evening sky, both from the boat and from the tube. Then it was skiing. I remember the girl who had never skied before. The apprehension that filled her face as she crouched in the water was replaced by ecstasy as she got up and skied behind the boat. When she clambered back into the boat, her face wasn't large enough to contain her grin.

I remember the boy who tried six times to get up—and failed. I remember the pats on the back and the expressions of support when he climbed into the boat, exhausted and discouraged. "You'll make it next time," someone said. "Just rest a little."

And an hour later he did make it.

Something happened in those three hours in the boat. We didn't give Bible studies, didn't even have a *Steps to Christ* along. But young people learned that their church cared about them, learned that God loved them, learned that Jesus gave His life to them. I was ministering to those teenagers.

Something else happened in the boat every Tuesday night. My tension melted. My frustration subsided. Joy returned to my life. The things that were so important at the office faded. Those teenagers ministered to me.

Every Tuesday afternoon that summer I regretted my time commitment to the young people of the church. But every Tuesday evening by 9 p.m., I was refreshed. I had a new perspective of what was—is—important.

And the next spring when the church asked for volunteers to bring boats to Water Fun Night every Tuesday night, I signed up.

"He is like a tree planted by streams of water, that yields its fruit in its season, and its leaf does not wither. In all that he does, he prospers." (Psalm 1:3, RSV).

# We All Know about Fragmentation

Ann Caulkins

"In a fragmented world, we serve society by raising our children in a healthy, cooperative community. Where home, church, and school work together to provide a consistent voice, children can grow into balanced, mature adults able to love God and care about others."[1]

We all know about fragmentation.
    Our busy lives attest to it.

    But we also seek that "consistent voice"
of home, church, and school where our children
    can learn to grow and work together.

    It starts with us.
They can learn cooperative community
from us.

They hear us discussing, encouraging, ana-
lyzing,
    giving and supporting one another—
    the construction sounds of community.

    The children watch us
Replacing, repairing, rebuilding—
    giving with a purpose...

More than buildings are repaired.
And the measure of our building together
    will be felt
        as they, in turn,
            Give...

    Which is more blessed.

[1] Risk and Promise Report, ValueGenesis Study, 1992.

# The Soaking Wet Gift

Tom Neslund

Eric's riveted eyes tried to push the hands of the clock forward. His brow creased with concentration. Only three more minutes until recess. He could make it. He had to make it. He knew the teacher wouldn't let him go to the bathroom with only three minutes until the recess bell. His classmates had tried that trick before, so they could get the best sports equipment. Only two and a half more minutes.

His teacher noticed Eric's new infatuation with the clock's second hand. She knew he wanted to be first into the gymnasium. "Eric," she called sharply. That was all it took for Eric to completely lose hold of his concentration and his little bladder.

And he just couldn't stop.

A puddle began to form in the dip of his chair. In seconds it would run over the sides and his classmates would know that Eric had wet his pants. The embarrassment would surely kill him. How could he face the teasing he'd hear for the rest of the school year?

Eric looked at the clock again. This time he tried to hold the hands back. He didn't want recess to come. He wanted time to stop. Even go backwards. But the second hand ticked quickly on. Eric remembered what his dad always told him. "Eric, if you're ever in trouble, the first thing you should do is pray." Right there Eric closed his eyes and offered his simple plea. "God, I'm in big trouble. Please do something. Please help me."

Opening his eyes, Eric saw Caroline coming down the aisle carrying the large classroom fishbowl. Shocked, he watched as she stumbled over her own feet right in front of him, completely drenching him with water and a flopping goldfish. Eric leaped to his feet sputtering, "Caroline, you clumsy idiot! How could you...? I can't believe you...." Shamefaced, Caroline shuffled out of the room, the jeers of her classmates following her. Eric went to the bathroom to dry off.

Eric immediately felt guilty. The accident had been just what he needed at the moment. But why did Caroline have to be embarrassed instead of him? He knew he had to apologize. Stopping Caroline after school, Eric began to stutter, "I'm sorry, Caroline. I had no right to yell at you and let all the other kids laugh." Eric couldn't bring himself to tell her that she was an answer to his prayer. "Please accept an apology from me," he finally said.

"That's okay, Eric. I know what it's like," Caroline replied. "I once wet my pants in class too."

# No Price Tag Attached

Rikki Stenbakken Welch

Ever since I read that story in ninth grade, I've wanted to help. The man in the story couldn't read, but he was really good at bluffing it. That is, he bluffed it until one day he was out in the garden and couldn't read the directions on how to get his nitro-glycerine tablets open and he died. It was awful. I wasn't the same for days. I told myself that if I ever had the chance to help somebody learn to read, I would.

So that's what I do. Every Tuesday night I meet with Mike, a thirty-something blue-collar worker with a fierce desire to read. We discuss short vowel sounds, long vowel sounds, and consonant blends.

Every week when we meet, I help him peel back a layer of mystery shrouding syllables, words, sentences, and paragraphs. Last week we spent almost half the time talking about the silent "e" and how it can turn a cut into something cute, or a hat into hate, or rip into ripe. I felt a special little sense of satisfaction when he learned to recognize one of my very favorite words—sale. I never realized a silent "e" could be so exciting.

Progress is slow, and some weeks I feel like I'm adding layers to the mystery rather than removing them. But there is progress. When he reads several sentences out of his phonics book without making a mistake, I know there's progress. When he sounds out a compound word like prizefighter (did you catch the silent "e"?) I know there's progress. I feel so proud. (I wonder if this is how my mother feels...)

Every week Mike thanks me for helping him. Not just an off-the-cuff "Hey thanks," but a genuine I-can't-believe-you're-doing-this-for-me sort of thank you. It's not like I'm handing him a roll of dollar bills or a new car. I'm giving him my time. I'm sharing my skill. I feel privileged. It makes me feel like I've done something worthwhile.

It gives me tingles to know that I can change someone's life. Maybe not revolutionize it, but change it nonetheless. A roll of bills won't take away the fear that he'll lose his job if someone finds out he's illiterate. But by meeting with him for an hour a week, I'm chipping away at that fear. I know I am, and I like knowing that.

Somehow, I don't think it would be the same if he were paying me for it. There's something exceptionally satisfying about knowing you're giving to someone. No price tag attached. It makes me feel like a real Christian. And I like that.

# A Bit of Myself in Your Favor

Dick Duerksen

A big box of candy sits in the work-room, a handwritten note beside it. The note reads, "Please buy some of this stuff so my kid can be on the basketball team." When I walk past the receptionist I see a box of wrapping paper. This time another parent says, "You've got to buy wrapping paper anyway, how about helping out my children?" Then there is the sign out in front of our elementary school. "Florida cit-rus," it shouts. "Get your order in today for winter delivery."

Am I giving when I buy the sugar-filled chocolate, wrap with special too-expensive paper, or drink the Florida orange juice? Or is philanthropy something different from the consumerism of fund raising?

My life is filled with people who gave to me without thinking about what they were receiving in the process. People whose giv-ing buttons were pressed more by needs than by candy and wrapping paper.

Like Glen, the giant-handed man who gave hours of his weekend time to teach several of us guys how to make the best model cars in town.

Like Grandpa Duerksen, who gave me his ancient Nash Rambler—long before I could legally drive. He smiled knowingly and encouraged me to "sell the car and use the money to do something that will make someone happy."

Like the anonymous person who sent me letters when I was an academy principal. The note would always read, "Please use this to make a student's life easier." Behind the note would be several $50s or a couple of $100s or, once, $1,000 in cash.

Like Ivan Angell, who quietly gave a piece of Dominican Republic land to provide a home for an orphanage.

Like Don Kirkman, who gave up the last seat on the San Salvador-to-Managua flight so a teacher could celebrate victory with a group of student church builders.

Like my wife, Brenda, who became a special kind of giver on the streets of Hong Kong. The outstretched hand of a blind beggar caused heavy stress on Brenda's heart, and on her nearly empty pocket-book. Unwilling to give just a coin, Brenda purchased a banana from a street vendor and rushed back up the street to the blind beggar. "Here, this is for you." She wrapped the hungry fingers around the golden fruit. For a brief second the woman caressed the banana, her face creased with amazement. Then, without a thank you, she sank to the ground, peeled the treasure, and enjoyed the feast.

Yes, I give when I buy the Florida citrus and the wrapping paper. But giving can be far more than exchanging coins for consumer goods. The greatest giving happens when I give a bit of myself in your favor.

# Popcorn Love

Doug Lawson

Not long ago I was having one of those days you would like to forget when I found myself at the door to my home. My sour face was suddenly confronted with seemingly unending kisses from an eight-pound bundle of fur named Popcorn. I didn't want these kisses, but they wouldn't stop. The more I tried to keep my sour look, the more Popcorn was all over me. In fact, he didn't stop until I laughed and gave that little white Maltese dog a hug.

As I continued into the house, my whole attitude changed. In fact, I forgot everything bad about the day. My facial expression was changed and so was the evening. It became one of the warmest, most fun evenings ever.

What Popcorn did for me we can do for others every day. He gave me what I didn't know I needed. He gave me unconditional love just when I needed it. I was down, but his love was up. I was sour, but his love was funny, fuzzy, and wet. He wanted to make me happy because he was so happy himself. He wanted me to know how much he loved me regardless of what mood I was in that minute on that day.

We all need "Popcorn Love" every day, especially when we are down. But how are we going to receive Popcorn Love when we need it?

We will receive it by giving it to others.

If we love the unlovable, the sour faces, especially when we are ourselves down, they will give us back what Popcorn gave me—my smile.

Love is something we do, not something we think about. Popcorn loved me all over my face and he got back my smile and a hug. That is what he wanted and he got it. That's what we need too, isn't it?

Unconditional love. And we can get it any minute of any day by deciding like Popcorn to give it first to others.

# We Value What We Chase

Mary Jane Mapes

"How do you determine your values?" asked a young woman recently in one of my training seminars. My response might have appeared too spontaneous, but in hindsight, I still believe it to be accurate.

"Simple," I said. "You know what you value by taking a look at what you chase, the diligence with which you chase it, and the joy you experience once you get it."

For example, I helped my son move out of his college dormitory at the end of the semester. In packing up his things, I noticed a jar candle (the dime-store type often found on backyard picnic tables). Inside the jar, melted into the wax, were lots of pennies. I asked, "Hey, Joey, don't you want this money?"

"Naw," he said, "it's only pennies." I quickly concluded that he didn't value money (not a good sign to me), and said so.

"Mom," he pleaded, "if it were quarters in that jar, I'd take the time to melt the wax and clean them out, but it's only pennies!" It made me think of the times I'd seen a penny on the street and never bothered to pick it up because it was a penny—little value.

However, I remember years ago taking my three-year-old daughter Lisa to the shopping mall at Christmas time. The mall was packed with people, mechanical toy displays, and extra retail booths brought in only for the holidays; we had to shout to be heard above the din.

In a major retail chain store, Lisa was at my side when I looked up to sort through a rack of blouses. When I looked down not more than 15 seconds later, she was gone. Mind and heart racing, I charged upstairs to find the woman on the PA system, all the way calling Lisa's name, my eyes frantically searching the store for my little girl. The woman upstairs didn't appear to share my concern for my lost daughter. She asked far too many questions—she was too slow. I had no time to wait. I had to find Lisa. Racing through the store, propriety aside, I began screaming her name. In retrospect, it's clear that I must have looked like a madwoman running through that store. Having always been a person for whom appearances mattered, it's interesting to note that then, as in childbirth, I didn't care who saw or heard me. Nothing was more important than finding my daughter.

I hadn't yet gotten out of the store when two women approached me and asked if I'd lost a little girl (wasn't it obvious!). "Yes, her name is Lisa. She's wearing a little red coat, blue corduroy pants and Mickey Mouse boots." I couldn't get the words out fast enough.

"Well, we found her in the middle of the mall crying. She wouldn't come with us because she said that her mother told her to never go with strangers. However, she was willing to wait at one of the center booths. Come with us, and we'll take you back to her."

From a distance I could see Lisa sitting on the counter of the booth, looking scared and tearful. When our eyes met, we exploded into tears. When I reached the booth, we threw our arms around each other and hung on for dear life. Thank God. My daughter was safe, and I was jubilant! In that moment, nothing else mattered.

Though some values change with time, the litmus test is to examine what we go after, the diligence with which we pursue it, and the joy we experience once it is within our grasp.

# What God Cannot Do

Peter, James, and John—alias: Jackie Bragaw

The last thing we wanted to do was fish. But that's what Jesus wanted us to do. We had fished all night and wanted to go home and get some sleep.

It had been a long night. We threw our nets into the water so many times our backs and necks ached. Now, this morning, just as we were getting ready to leave the boat, we noticed a crowd coming towards us with Jesus in the lead. He smiled and waved, "Quite a crowd wouldn't you say?" he called.

Jesus stopped at the water's edge and began speaking to the people. As more people came they pressed in on Jesus so that he had to back into the water. When he was about knee-deep, we realized we ought to do something. So we pulled the boat over and he hopped aboard and kept talking.

When Jesus finished speaking he turned

and said something quite ridiculous. He said, "Push off. Let's go catch some fish."

We groaned. We didn't mind him using the boat as a stage, but we weren't too excited about going back out into the lake again to fish. We'd been out there all night with no results. Jesus was an excellent carpenter and teacher, but we were the fishermen.

We tried to explain to Jesus how our luck had been last night, but he just grinned and said, "Please." How could we say no? So with a grunt we shoved off. We shook our heads as we rowed. "This is impossible, you know. We may not know much, but we are professional fishermen."

Finally, Jesus decided we had come to the right place—like it would make a difference in broad daylight—and told us to drop anchor and throw out the nets. So we did. As we were ready to drop the nets over we looked skeptically at Jesus. He was just standing there smiling—the kind of excited smile you see on someone's face as they hand you a gift they know you're going to love.

We hated to disappoint him, but what could we do? So we dropped the nets and started to settle in for a long wait. But there was no wait. The ropes jerked taut the minute they sank and the boat started to roll over on its side. We pulled the net in as fast as we could, which was no easy feat. Once we had hauled in the nets, the boat sat so low it began to take on water. We called for another boat and it came.

Here we were: a bunch of fishermen, two boats, knee-deep in fish, and Jesus, sitting in the bow grinning. That's when it hit us who He really was. And then we realized who we really were. We were fishermen telling God what He couldn't do.

# Community Service Day

Roy Wu

One of my greatest memories of college was the opportunity I had to serve as a representative in student government. It was such a strong feeling of pride, knowing I had been given the responsibility to represent my peers.

Student government is a unique opportunity to work with others to develop ideas that will benefit other students. We wanted to do more than plan parties and banquets.

One of our goals was to find some way for the students to be more involved with the local community. But what could we do to make an impact on *our* community? We were busy college students. How would we go about building relations between our school and the community? These were just a few of the questions that came up as we pieced together some sort of community event.

But we pushed ahead with a plan for

Community Service Day for Columbia Union College. Students would have the day off from classes to literally clean up the town. Well, Community Service Day was a great idea, but would it work out for us? Would we have sponsorship? Would the faculty actually give us the time off from school? Would anybody show up and participate?

The faculty did give us the time and we worked with the city Department of Works and assembled a group of students, faculty, and staff to do a variety of jobs. Slowly everything came together, just as we planned.

The day came and people arrived to take part. Armed with gloves, shovels, rakes, and buckets, different groups of students cleaned and landscaped a local park, painted curbs, mulched flower beds, and swept the streets.

There we were, Columbia Union College, down on its hands and knees getting dirty to clean up our town. And we made it happen. The student leaders had worked together to make this event because we believed in our school. We wanted to be a part of the local community, and we had a part to play in building up our town.

The mayor commended us with a citation of appreciation at a town hall meeting. And the college faculty approved an annual Community Service Day.

I thought this event would teach me all there is to know about developing ties with a community. But I realize now I have a long way to go. It didn't matter if people saw us out working. It didn't matter if only 10 people showed up to work. What mattered was that we were actually doing something to benefit our community.

# Giving a Year of My Life

Amy Fisher

I gave away a year of my life when I decided to take a year out of college and serve as a teacher in the islands of Palau. I taught 21 sixth graders in a small concrete classroom with a blackboard and temperamental electricity.

Most days I felt inadequate for the job. I knew I lacked patience and knowledge for my task. The kids were at a tough age. They no longer looked up to their teacher as the only source of knowledge, but instead found it almost enjoyable to challenge me. I struggled with discipline and to keep them on task, some days simply sitting with them after school so they could finish their schoolwork.

Today, as I sit on the floor of my room and look through the journal that recorded my thoughts during those months, I realize I did more than struggle, I grew. I'm still not sure if I taught them everything they should know about inertia, the history of Latin America, or fractions, but I know that because I gave my time, they gave me a new way to look at the world.

## Journal entry: June 6, 1996

The last day of school went well. I'm glad it's over. Complete relief. What a wonderful feeling. I cleaned up. Swept up the last dust from the corners, washed the finger smudges off the walls, and stacked the desks in a corner. I signed the last year-book, took the last wad of tape off the bulletin boards. I listened to the echo as I shut the door and locked it for the last time. As I passed the window, I looked into the room where I dedicated a year of my life. One year doesn't seem long now.

I told my principal that I'm glad I taught sixth grade and I meant it. I think sometimes I learned more in that dusty classroom than I could teach. I learned patience. I learned about kids. I learned the impact we can have on each other's lives. I'm not sad to leave this classroom, but when I think of my students I know I will miss them. Shannon grinned from ear to ear today when I told her that all her work paid off and she could go on to seventh grade. She taught me perseverance. I love her. "Thank you, Miss Fisher," she said as she hugged me.

You can be changed by helping others. I've always heard this but never truly believed it until I gave 10 months of my life on a small island in Micronesia to a group of sixth graders in Palau.

I scrawled a Chinese proverb that I found in the pages of my journal that reminds me why giving is so important. It says, "A bit of fragrance always clings to the hand that gives you roses." If I look closely, I can still feel the parts of Palau that cling to me. I feel Shannon's hug, the high five from Michael, and the wave from Lizzy as the students ran out the small concrete classroom and into the sweltering Palauan sunlight. For them, it was the end of a school year and the promise of a long summer. For me, it was the end of my year in Palau and the promise of a life of learning through giving.

# Love Lifted Me

Justin Dart, Jr.

*This article is taken from a speech Justin Dart, Jr. gave for the annual Presidents' Dinner for Philanthropy at the Adventist World Headquarters.*

I was born in 1930, in a Chicago family of wealthy, media-prominent winners. My father was a college football star, a super-successful business executive and conservative political activist who would advise several presidents. My mother combined movie star good looks, wealth, and a genius IQ to become a prominent author and a national leader in avant garde politics, literature, and art.

Poles apart, my parents were divorced early on, in an atmosphere of hostility which totally dominated my childhood.

Surrounded by hostile "super winners," I decided that the only way to establish my own identity was to be a hostile "super loser." I never met a person I couldn't insult. I never met a rule or an object I couldn't break.

Family friends issuing invitations to my mother and father learned to say, "but don't bring Justin."

I went to seven high schools, graduating from none. Along the way I broke Humphrey Bogart's all-time demerit record.... People didn't like me. I didn't like myself.

In 1948, at age 18, I was living with my father in California when I contracted polio. The doctors at Los Angeles County Hospital told my parents I would die in a few days, but not to worry, I would be better off dead than crippled.

My father's answer could not be repeated in this company. He did some quick research and found a hospital operated by people to whom each human life was sacred. The White Memorial Hospital operated by the College of Medical Evangelists—by the Seventh-day Adventist Church. By you.

This was something new for me—being with people who were passionately dedicated to expressing love for each other, for me—even though I was rude to them. These people seemed so happy. I could feel the warmth of their love. It was a good feeling.

I thought, Justin, if you are only going to live a few more days, why not try this love thing—try smiling and being positive. For the first time I knew the joy of life. I sort of went wild experimenting with love.

I have vivid memories of singing hymns with my nurses—when nothing else would help, "Love Lifted Me." And it did. It did. The love—and the passionate, loving science—of these strangers saved my life.

Far more importantly, they resurrected my spirit, the sick spirit of a young man who had lived a short, lonesome lifetime of failure, hostility, and self-hate.

It soon became apparent that I was not going to die, but that I would be a wheelchair user for the rest of my life. There was no period of grieving. I count the happy, the valuable, the responsible days of my life from the first week I was exposed to the magnificent, dedicated, loving people at White Memorial Hospital. And what a magnificent life you have given me.

There were so many beautiful people. I remember particularly my doctor, Joseph E. Maschmeyer—trained at the Mayo Clinic, a specialist in physical medicine.

He was not a handsome or charming man. Skinny, red faced, bulgy eyes, collars too big—he looked like the bumbling store clerk in a comedy movie. He was simply the most loving, dedicated, truthful, and brilliant man I had ever met. I called him Uncle Joe.

Tragically, he developed terminal cancer as a relatively young man—a few years after I left the hospital. I promised him I would carry on the good fight.

When I came out of the hospital I was 20, a new wheel chairuser, faced by a society where there was apparently no place for me. With my disability, and my miserable academic record, no college would accept me. Except yours—La Sierra College near Los Angeles. Again the power of love lifted me.

One of my classmates was H.M.S. Richards, a big, strong, handsome man who became a loving, tough older brother helping me with my rehabilitation exercises and studies, collecting money to pay my tuition when my family objected to a small Christian college.

For the first time I worked hard and got

good grades. I qualified for the University of Houston, where I received a B.S. and M.A. with an A average.

What an honor, what a happiness to be here tonight with you, who have done so much for me. Thanks to patriots past, thanks to patriots present, thanks to you in this room tonight, America is the richest, most productive and democratic nation in history.

Americans with disabilities have come a long way—the ADA declares us full citizens. But the job of democracy is far from finished. Millions of people with and without disabilities, in America and other lands, are still outcasts from the good life. No person, rich or poor, is living as well as they could.

There are about one billion people with disabilities in the world. The world's poorest, most oppressed, welfare-dependent group—67 percent unemployed in this country, millions who can't get health insurance for any price, unless they go on welfare. In many countries we are beggars or incarcerated in concentration camp-like institutions. There are still countries where they kill babies with disabilities.

How many million people with disabilities die every year from violence, from lack of the basic necessities of life? Two million? Four million? Ten million?

Nobody knows. Dead whales they count. Spotted owls and butterflies they count. Deaths among people with disabilities they don't even bother to count. Holocaust.

Now we Americans have the potential to utilize the unlimited force of science and free enterprise democracy to eliminate poverty, discrimination, violence, and ignorance—to empower every American to live the human dream.

Will we do it, or will we, like so many great cultures past, relax in the status quo, and go down the road of self-indulgence and disunity to the land of might have been?

The world is watching American democracy. The world will follow what we do. Failure is unthinkable.

Today I present to you what I passionately believe is the most important issue for America, the most important issue for humanity now. Empowerment.

In 1776 the issue was the inalienable

rights of all people. Today it is empowerment of all people to exercise those rights and the responsibilities that go with them.

I am convinced that we will never achieve full, productive participation for any American until there is a revolution to establish a culture that systematically empowers all to live their God-given potential.

Empowerment. What is it?

Empowerment is when we understand that people with disabilities are not a tragic minority. We are a triumphant majority. Modern medicine and rehabilitation have enabled millions to triumph over death, and to live happy, productive lives with disabilities.

There are 54 million Americans with disabilities. Seven of 10 Americans will have a disability at some point during their lives. Every American family will experience a disability.

Public policy, business policy, or religion that doesn't meet the needs of people with disabilities doesn't meet the needs of anyone.

Empowerment is when we understand that the legitimate purpose of society, its governments, and its institutions, is not to govern people, not to provide the good life for them, but to empower them to govern themselves and to provide the good life for themselves.

Empowerment is when we understand that inalienable rights are inseparable from inalienable responsibilities. Each one of us is inescapably responsible to participate in democratic government, to invest all of our abilities and resources in producing lives of quality for ourselves and for all. For all. For all.

You cannot be responsible for your own family without being responsible for the society in which they live. And that's what you are doing here tonight. Taking responsibility.

Empowerment is when we understand that the client of medical and social services deserves no less efficiency, respect, and choice than the client of Merrill Lynch.

Empowerment is when we understand that the productivity, the prosperity, the quality of life of a child with cerebral palsy is just as important as that of the president of the United States.

Our experiments with empowerment

have created the explosive success of free enterprise democracy. We recognize this in rhetoric. It is time to move from rhetoric and experiment to the systematic empowerment of all.

Healthcare that empowers all, education, rehabilitation that empowers all, transportation, communication, communities that empower all. Social security, welfare that empowers all who can work to do it, and empowers all who cannot work to live in dignity. Religion that empowers all. These are some of the foundational concepts of a culture that empowers.

But can we afford to create the empowerment culture. We can't afford *not* to do it. The status quo is creating the deficits and the poverty gap.

Systematic, aggressive empowerment by individuals, families, businesses, churches, and government will dramatically lower the overhead and increase the productivity and quality of American life. It will create millions of new jobs.

There will be an economic boom that will dwarf the industrial revolution. America will renew its economic and moral leadership of the world.

Empowerment, America, is possible. We have the money, the talent, the technology. But do we have the will?

Who will make the dream live?

Look around this gathering. The buck stops here.

We have done much. We have to do more.

But how can we possibly overcome the ancient stereotypes, the powerful lobbies for the status quo?

Not with business as usual. Our most powerful enemy is not the special interests and their millions. It is apathy. It is cynicism. It is the temptation to say, "It's all too much. Nothing I do will make a difference. I'll put in my nine to five. I'll put in my five volunteer hours. Somehow things will work out."

History is clear. Things do not work themselves out. Spectators lose. Spectator cultures perish. People willing to lay their lives on the line win.

If enough of us, a critical mass, are willing to pledge our lives, our fortunes, and our sacred honor—if we are willing to make real sacrifices, to go to our personal Valley Forges—and to stay there for however long it takes, we can prevail.

Let us each one, reach into the depths of our beings.

Let us unite in action.

We of the disability community, you of the Adventist church, know about empowerment. We can lead, and we must.

Get into empowerment as if your lives depended on it. They do. And the lives of your children, the lives of all humans in the 21st century.

The war for a responsible America will be won or lost in your church, your hospital, your university, your living room.

My words are inadequate. Listen to the heart of this old soldier. In the twilight of my life, I agonize over my responsibility to you, to America, to all humans, present and future. I raise my passionate prayer for the will, the wisdom, the courage to transcend my weaknesses and give all that I am.

And I thank God for you. You have created miracles in the lives of thousands—in my life.

The night before Martin Luther King, Jr. was murdered, he said, "I do not fear death, mine eyes have seen the glory."

I am no Martin Luther King, but mine

eyes have seen the glory. It is not the titles and the awards you read about in the program.

Mine eyes have seen the glory. It is you. It is us together when we have achieved oneness struggling to live the great commandment of our God—that ye love one another as I have loved you.

I reach out to each one of you. I ask for your guidance and your inspiration. I ask for the privilege of spending the rest of my years fighting at your side as a citizen soldier for a revolution of love that empowers. Uncle Joe, I am here. Lift me one more time.

Beloved colleagues, you of the Adventist church have a great vision. You have a great record. You have great people. You have a record of loving empowerment. You can lead us to the Promised Land.

We of the disability community are with you—54 million strong, plus millions more, our families and advocates. Our infant movement is growing. We have much to learn. We have something to teach. Guide us. Listen to us. Invest in us.

We'll give you return for the dollar and the dedication. We won't all become

The Ministry of Philanthropy

Adventists, but we'll give you passion for love and justice that can't be bought for money.

And although I am not an Adventist, I urge you to support Adventist philanthropy. There is no better way to advance the American dream and the agenda of God. Let us embrace and lift each other. Let us reject hostility, self-indulgence, and retreat. Let us go forward together in the great tradition of Washington, Jefferson, Lincoln, Martin Luther King, Ellen White, and Joe Maschmeyer. Let us greet intimidation with courage, hate with love, demagoguery with simple truth. Let us overwhelm fear and fallacy and escapism with our vision of an America that empowers all.

Let us unite to empower America, men and women, young and old, people with and without disabilities, Republicans, Democrats, and Independents, business, labor, rich, poor, and middle class.

Let us unite to empower America, blacks, whites, browns, immigrants and natives, gays and lesbians, Christians, Muslims and Jews, pro-lifers and pro-choicers. Every American has a valuable contribution to make.

107

We're going to win. We're going to live the dream. I believe that because I believe in you. I owe you so much. I love you so much.

Let us shout together, each in our own way. America, join us in keeping the sacred pledge: one nation under God, indivisible, with liberty and justice for all.

# The Selfish Flashlight

Jeff Scoggins

In the storage yard behind a successful factory, lived stacks of sheet metal which were used to construct lanterns and flashlights. The factory made all sizes and kinds of lanterns. And flashlights ran the full range from tiny penlights to fit in a shirt pocket, to long Maglights.

Sometimes at night the sheet metal behind the factory would discuss how they would shine when they became lanterns. It was every piece of sheet metal's dream to become a lantern. Lanterns had so much light that they could give a lot of it and still have plenty left for themselves. No one really wanted to be a flashlight. When compared to the lanterns, their light was feeble and only shone in one spot. There was not much glory in the job of a flashlight.

Over time the pieces of metal were taken into the factory where some were made into lanterns and others into flashlights. The flashlights were given their batteries and put on a shelf in a room to await shipment to the stores. On the opposite wall where all could see was a large sign, written by the owner of the factory, describing what the flashlights were to do after they were purchased at the store. Considering how the flashlights felt about not being created lanterns, one command in particular made them especially angry. It said, "Give your light. It is why you were made." The last line said simply, "I love my lanterns and flashlights. I will take care of you."

But the flashlights complained among themselves, especially the little penlights. "How can we do any good with the little bit of light we give?"

"We will be completely unappreciated when people see the bright light of the lanterns," said the bigger flashlights.

"Besides, our batteries run down. We can feel it every time we get switched on," said the Maglights. "Pretty soon we will be empty, and then what!?"

So some of the flashlights decided they would not work at all anymore. A few others decided they would work only in an emergency. Still others decided they would work only when they were banged around and virtually forced to shine. But a few flashlights decided that if the owner really loved them like he said he did, that they would trust him to look out for them and they would go ahead and give the best light they could, just as he asked.

Well, soon the flashlights were shipped out to the stores to be sold. Usually shoppers would try the flashlights before they bought them and they would skip over any that didn't work. After a few weeks in the store the flashlights that refused to give their light began to get a little lonely. Only when a shopper bought a flashlight without trying it first did the stubborn ones get bought at all. And that was even worse, because when a shopper bought a flashlight and then found that it didn't work, they either immediately returned it to the store, which was a great embarrassment for the flashlight, or they put it in a dark closet all by itself and forgot about it.

One such flashlight, bought by mistake, was particularly stubborn. He clenched his wires so tight that his batteries began to corrode. But that was better than running out of voltage, he thought to himself as he lay shivering in his dark closet.

Then one night came a terrible thunderstorm, and the electricity in the house where this flashlight lived went out. He heard someone coming down the hall for him, and he began to clench his wires. But then in the darkness the baby began to cry in fear, and something inside the selfish flashlight made him relax his wires just a little. Maybe just this one time he'd help out and give a little light. After all, he was all they had right now.

The family cheered when he switched on, and he felt a shiver go through him. He also felt his batteries begin to drain, but oh boy was it worth it! The light he was giving, which he thought was so little and so worthless, was making this family very happy. He just might have to try shining his light a little more often. And that's just what the flashlight did. Soon he found himself going on camping trips, to visit the neighbors, and all kinds of other neat stuff. He began to realize that the more light he gave, the more life he got back. He was happy!

And his batteries did run out. But you know what? He was given brand new ones. The owner did care after all.